INSIDE
VOLCANOES

by Melissa Stewart
Illustrations throughout by Cynthia Shaw

STERLING CHILDREN'S BOOKS
New York

STERLING CHILDREN'S BOOKS
New York

An Imprint of Sterling Publishing
387 Park Avenue South
New York, NY 10016

STERLING CHILDREN'S BOOKS and the distinctive Sterling Children's Books logo are registered trademarks of Sterling Publishing Co., Inc.

Library of Congress Cataloging-in-Publication Data Available

Lot#:
10 9 8 7 6 5 4 3 2 1
03/11
Published by Sterling Publishing Co., Inc.
387 Park Avenue South, New York, NY 10016

www.sterlingpublishing.com/kids

© 2011 by Melissa Stewart
Distributed in Canada by Sterling Publishing
c/o Canadian Manda Group, 165 Dufferin Street
Toronto, Ontario, Canada M6K 3H6
Distributed in the United Kingdom by GMC Distribution Services
Castle Place, 166 High Street, Lewes, East Sussex, England BN7 1XU
Distributed in Australia by Capricorn Link (Australia) Pty. Ltd.
P.O. Box 704, Windsor, NSW 2756, Australia

Printed in China
All rights reserved.

Sterling ISBN 978-1-4027-5876-8 (hardcover)
          978-1-4027-8164-3 (flexibound)

For information about custom editions, special sales, premium and corporate purchases, please contact Sterling Special Sales Department at 800-805-5489 or specialsales@sterlingpublishing.com.

Designed by Anke Stohlmann Design.

IMAGE CREDITS:

Alamy: © Melinda Podor: 23 middle right

Corbis: © Arctic-Images: 18 bottom, 28 (3); © Atlantide Phototravel: 4-9; © Gary Braasch: 15 right; © Tony Craddock: 23 top; © Alberto Garcia: 37; © J. D. Griggs: 11 top; © HO/Reuters: 2-3, 28 (4), back cover; © Rob Howard: 39; © Steven Kazlowski/Science Faction: 35; © Douglas Kirkland: 36; © Frank Krahmer: 23 middle left; © G. Brad Lewis/Science Faction: 11 bottom left; © J.P. Lockwood: 14 bottom left; © Imelda Medina/epa: 14 top; NASA: 6, 41; © Roger Ressmeyer: 1, 26, 28 (0), 38; © Martin Rietze/Westend61: 12 right; © Scientifica/Visuals Unlimited: 25 top right; © George Steinmetz: 23 bottom; © Jim Sugar/Science Faction: 12 left; © Steve Terrill: 34 bottom; © Mike Zens: 19 top

© 2011 Cynthia Shaw: All maps and diagrams

Getty Images: 18 top © Simon Russell

iStockphoto.com: © AquaColor: 25 bottom left; © Jesus Ayala: 26 bottom right; © Sean Curry: 22 top left; © Mark Higgins: 22 top right; © JJRD: 22 bottom right; © Matthew Jones: 22 bottom left; © Vladimir Piskunov: 28 (1); © Patrick Roherty: 28 (2); © Danny Warren: 25 top left

© Ron Miller: 44 (Neptune)

NASA: 28 (7), 31, 44 (all except Jupiter, Neptune)

National Oceanic and Atmospheric Administration: 43

National Park Service: Craters of the Moon National Monument and Preserve: 11 bottom right and 14 bottom right

Photolibrary: © Bernhard Edmaier/Look-foto/Photolibrary: front cover; © Ed Reschke/Peter Arnold Images: 10; © Japan Travel Bureau: 19 bottom left

Photo Researchers, Inc.: © Hoa-Qui: 28 (6); © Images & Volcans: 19 bottom right; © Krafft/Explorer: 40; NASA/Science Source: 44 (Jupiter); © Stephen & Donna O'Meara: 11 bottom middle

© Taro Taylor: 15 left

USGS: 28 (5); 34 top

BURNING MOUNTAIN

Volcanoes all over the world have spewed lava and ash for billions of years, so it's no surprise that the name we use to describe these "burning mountains" has ancient origins.

More than 2,000 years ago, the Romans used the Latin word *Vulcanus* when talking about Mount Etna. They believed that Vulcan, the Roman god of fire and metalworking, had his workshop at the top of the 10,900-foot (3,300-meter) tall volcanic mountain. Whenever the volcano erupted, the Romans said Vulcan was making weapons for Mars, the Roman god of war.

Today, Mount Etna, located on the Italian island of Sicily, is the largest volcano in Europe and one of the most active on Earth. Its 2002–2003 eruption, shown here, lasted nearly four months.

A CRACK IN THE EARTH

Layers of Earth

When someone says *volcano*, you probably picture a tall mountain, like Mount Etna, rising into the sky. But many volcanoes have gentle slopes covered by forests, and some are completely flat. At the heart of every volcano—whether it's big or small, steep or flat—is a crack that extends through Earth's uppermost layer, or crust, and into the mantle.

The mantle is the layer of Earth beneath the crust. It contains hot, soft rock called magma. Like cooked oatmeal, magma is thick, but it can flow.

The heat that keeps magma partially melted comes from Earth's fiery core. Underneath the mantle layer is the outer core. The melted metals in the outer core are at least 6,700 degrees Fahrenheit (3,700 degrees Celsius). Inside the inner core, things are even hotter, but the inner core is made of solid metals. The weight of the three overlying layers—the crust, the mantle, and the outer core—presses down on the inner core. All that pressure holds the inner core's molecules so close together that they can't turn into a liquid.

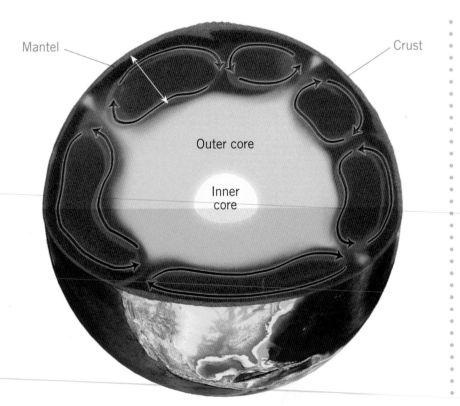

Mantel

Crust

Outer core

Inner core

Cool It!

When Earth formed 4.6 billion years ago, the entire planet was made of magma. It took millions of years for Earth to cool enough for its crust to harden.

The thin, outer layer of our planet is called the crust. The next layer, the mantle, contains magma that is always on the move. The core consists of an outer liquid layer and a solid inner layer.

Astronauts onboard the Space Shuttle *Endeavour* photographed this stunning view of ash erupting from Russia's Kliuchevskoi Volcano in 1994.

CONTENTS

How to read this book

This book is different from most you've read. Many of its pages fold out—or flip up! To know where to read next, follow arrows like these (⬆), and look for page numbers to help you find your place. Happy exploring!

Alive and Kickin'!

Mount Etna has erupted more than 210 times in recorded history. Since 2000, it has blown its top almost every year.

RIP AND SPLIT

In some parts of the world, plates are pulling apart. As they separate, magma rises to the surface and spills out as lava. It cools and hardens to form new seafloor and new land.

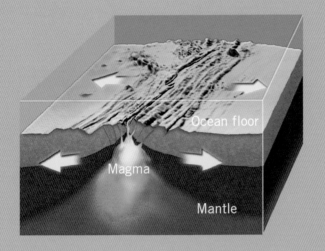

Ocean floor

Magma

Mantle

That's Incredible!

As the North American Plate and Eurasian Plate move in opposite directions, the Atlantic Ocean slowly gets wider. During your lifetime, the distance between Europe and North America will increase about 6 feet (2 m).

BUMP AND SLIDE

In other areas of the world, plates are crashing into one another. Sometimes one plate slides below the other and melts to form new magma. Some of that magma forces its way up through Earth's crust and erupts out of cracks on the planet's surface. This is what's happening along the edges of the Pacific Plate. So many volcanoes are located in this region that scientists call it the Pacific Ring of Fire.

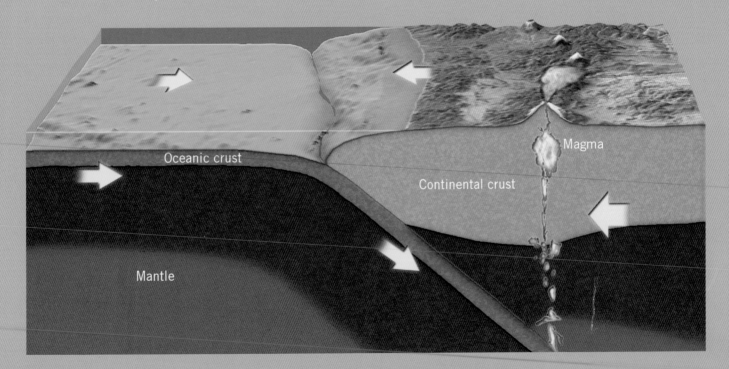

Oceanic crust

Magma

Continental crust

Mantle

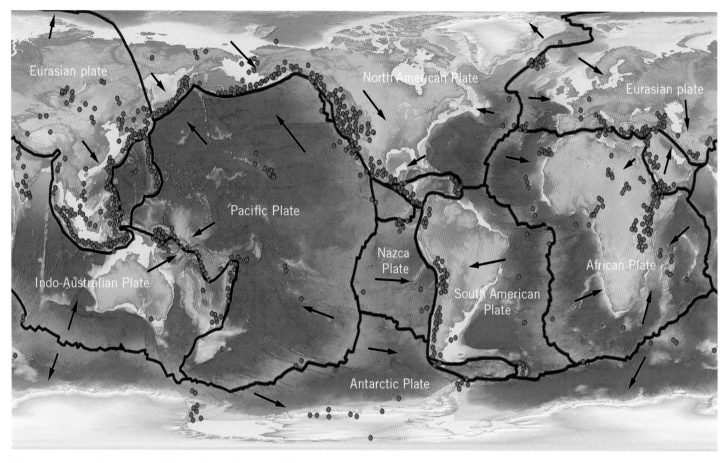

As you can see from the pattern of red dots on this map, most volcanoes are located along the edges of tectonic plates.

Land on the Move

Volcanoes are not spread evenly over Earth's surface. They are most common along the edges of Earth's tectonic plates—giant slabs of rock that make up the crust. These plates float on top of the mantle like rafts on a sea of moving magma.

Earth's sizzling-hot core constantly releases heat into the cooler mantle. This flow of heat energy causes magma in the mantle to slowly swirl in giant circles. As the hot magma near the core moves up toward Earth's surface, cooler magma sinks down to take its place. It may take millions of years for the magma to complete one loop.

As magma circles through Earth's mantle, the plates go along for the ride. On average, Earth's plates move about 2 inches (5 centimeters) each year. Your fingernails grow at about the same rate.

Ahead of His Time

In 1912, a German scientist named Alfred Wegener noticed that some continents seem to fit together like the pieces of a jigsaw puzzle. He suggested that Earth's crust is made of moving plates. Scientists couldn't imagine what would cause land to move, so they rejected Wegener's theory. Now we know that Wegener was right.

Hot Spots

Most volcanoes form along the edges of plates, but the Hawaiian Islands are located smack dab in the middle of the Pacific Plate. That's because these islands formed as lava slowly leaked out of a hotspot—a place where magma spikes through Earth's crust in the middle of a plate—and built up over thousands of years. Eventually, the layers of lava rose above the waves to form land.

Hotspots don't move, but the land or seafloor above them does. Over time, hotspots create chains of islands or mountains. The same hotspot formed all the Hawaiian Islands, one after the other.

Scientists have found about fifty active hotspots all over the world. Many are located below the seafloor, like the Hawaiian Hotspot. But others are centered below land. For example, the Yellowstone Hotspot lies beneath Yellowstone National Park in the United States. The heat from the hotspot fuels all of the park's world-famous hot springs and geysers, including Old Faithful.

Old Faithful is one of three hundred geysers fueled by the Yellowstone Hotspot. Every 45 to 125 minutes, it blasts up to 8,400 gallons (32,000 liters) of boiling water into the air.

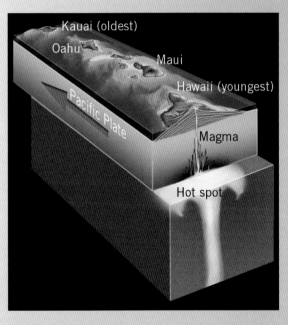

The Hawaiian Hotspot has been spewing out lava for more than 70 million years. During that time, it has formed at least 129 volcanoes, including the ones that make up the nineteen Hawaiian Islands. Kauai, the oldest island, was formed about 30 million years ago. The youngest island, Hawai'i, is still forming today.

Mauna Loa is one of five volcanoes that make up the island of Hawai'i. Measured from its base on the seafloor, Mauna Loa is nearly 6 miles (9.6 km) high, making it the second tallest mountain in the world. Mauna Loa first erupted between 700,000 and 1 million years ago, and it has been growing ever since. This image shows Mauna Loa's last eruption in 1984, but scientists think it could erupt again soon.

THREE KINDS OF LAVA

Most scientists divide lava into three different groups, based on how it flows and what its surface looks like when it cools.

Pahoehoe lava

This lava is thin and has a smooth surface. When pahoehoe cools, it forms rounded lobes, and the surface looks like a mass of twisted rope.

A'a lava

This lava is thicker and stickier than pahoehoe. When a'a cools, its surface is sharp and jagged.

Blocky lava

This lava is so thick that it usually doesn't travel very far. When it cools, it forms overlapping blocks of different sizes.

Volcanic ash

The thick volcanic ash you see here is made of tiny bits of lava that solidify as soon as they hit the air. Some of the powdery dust can be so fine that it becomes trapped in Earth's atmosphere. The rest of the ash drifts down and blankets the ground. Volcanic ash can clog the engines of cars and airplanes, destroy crops, and cause people to suffocate.

Volcano Popocatepetl in Mexico erupts spewing volcanic gas and ash.

Lapilli

Lapilli consists of pebble-sized pieces of volcanic rock that may rain down over a wide area of land. It can break windows and start forest fires. If enough lapilli piles up, it can cause roofs to collapse.

Volcanic bomb

A volcanic bomb, such as this one found at the Craters of the Moon National Monument in Idaho, is a large chunk of volcanic rock. It can be as small as a baseball or as large as a car. Volcanic bombs can be very dangerous,

WHAT A BLAST!

Four Kinds of Eruptions

Not all volcanic eruptions are the same. Sometimes a slow, steady stream of lava oozes out of a volcano for weeks, months, or years. Other blasts are more sudden and more explosive. That's why scientists have come up with four major categories, or types, of eruptions. To classify an eruption, scientists look at how violent it is and the kinds of material it produces.

Hawaiian

Fountains or rivers of lava flow out of the volcano in short, frequent bursts and spread out over a wide area of land.

Strombolian

These eruptions are a bit more violent, but they usually don't cause much damage to the surrounding land. They produce tall fountains of lava almost continuously and may throw some ash and rock into the air.

Kilauea Volcano, Hawaii

Fuego Volcano, Guatemala

Volcanic gas

Volcanic gas includes steam and other gases that may be harmful. Carbon dioxide can make breathing difficult for people and other animals. Sulfur dioxide can mix with gases in the air to create acid rain. Acid rain can damage trees, kill fish, and eat away at buildings and other stone structures. Fluorine and chlorine can damage the ozone layer, a thin layer of gases in Earth's atmosphere that blocks harmful rays from the sun.

Nearly all volcanic eruptions send lava oozing, gushing, or blasting onto Earth's surface. But lava isn't the only material volcanoes produce. Most blasts belch thick clouds of ash and steaming-hot gases. Some even hurl boulders high into the air.

Vulcanian

When gas builds up under thick, sticky lava, powerful blasts spew massive clouds of ash, lava, and rocks into the air. They are more violent and less frequent than Hawaiian and Strombolian eruptions.

Plinian

These super strong blasts empty all the lava and other materials inside a volcano. They belch giant clouds of ash and gases high into the sky. Sometimes deadly clouds of ash and gases race down the slopes of the volcano faster than a speeding car.

Tavurvur Volcano, Papua New Guinea

Mount St. Helens, Washington, United States

Mt. Ngauruhoe in New Zealand

1

Eyjafjallajokull, Iceland

2

Kinds of Volcanoes

Volcanoes can be many different shapes and sizes, from mounds with gentle slopes to giant, cone-shaped mountains. In fact, scientists have located more than two dozen kinds of volcanoes on Earth.

Why is there so much variety? Because a volcano's appearance depends on how forcefully it erupts and the kinds of materials it ejects.

After you read about the five major kinds of volcanoes, see if you classify each of the volcanoes shown in the photographs on pages 18 and 19. You'll find the answers on the bottom of page 20. Good luck!

Trick of the Trade

Scientists can classify a volcano even if they never see it erupt. By studying the land around the crater, they can figure out how violently it has erupted in the past and the kinds of material it has spewed into the sky.

Fissure Volcano

A fissure volcano is a long crack in Earth's surface. It gushes hot, very thin lava that spreads out so quickly it doesn't form a mound or mountain. Depending on the surrounding landscape, it may create a vast volcanic plain.

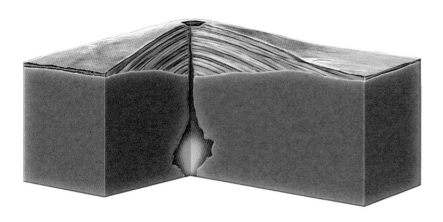

Shield Volcano

A shield volcano has a broad base with gently sloping sides. It forms when thin lava flows quickly and spreads over a fairly wide area.

INSIDE AND OUTSIDE VOLCANOES

Inside a Volcano

Have you ever wondered what the inside of a volcano looks like? Here's your chance to find out. Even though volcanoes come in many different shapes and sizes, they all have the same basic parts—a crater, a conduit, and a magma chamber.

Heat and pressure force magma and gases near the top of the mantle to rise up into cracks in Earth's crust. Slowly, the pent up fiery material pushes its way into the magma chamber of a volcano. When the heat and pressure inside the magma chamber are great enough, the material it holds suddenly rushes up the conduit and blasts, gushes, or oozes out of the crater. The volcano erupts!

Sizzling Sunsets

Following a volcanic eruption, people living near a volcano often enjoy beautiful sunsets. As the light of the sinking sun reflects off bits of ash in the air, the sky glows with brilliant pinks and reds.

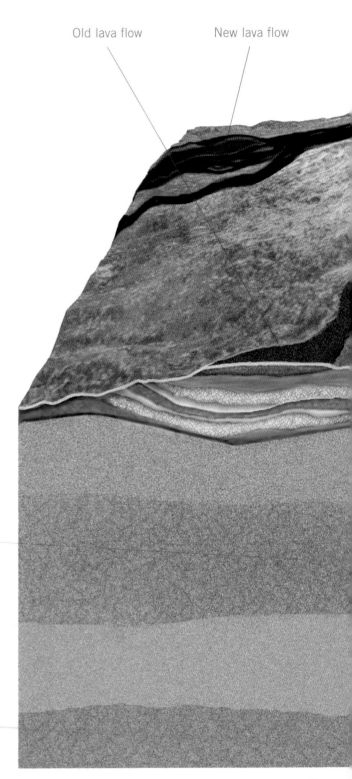

Old lava flow   New lava flow

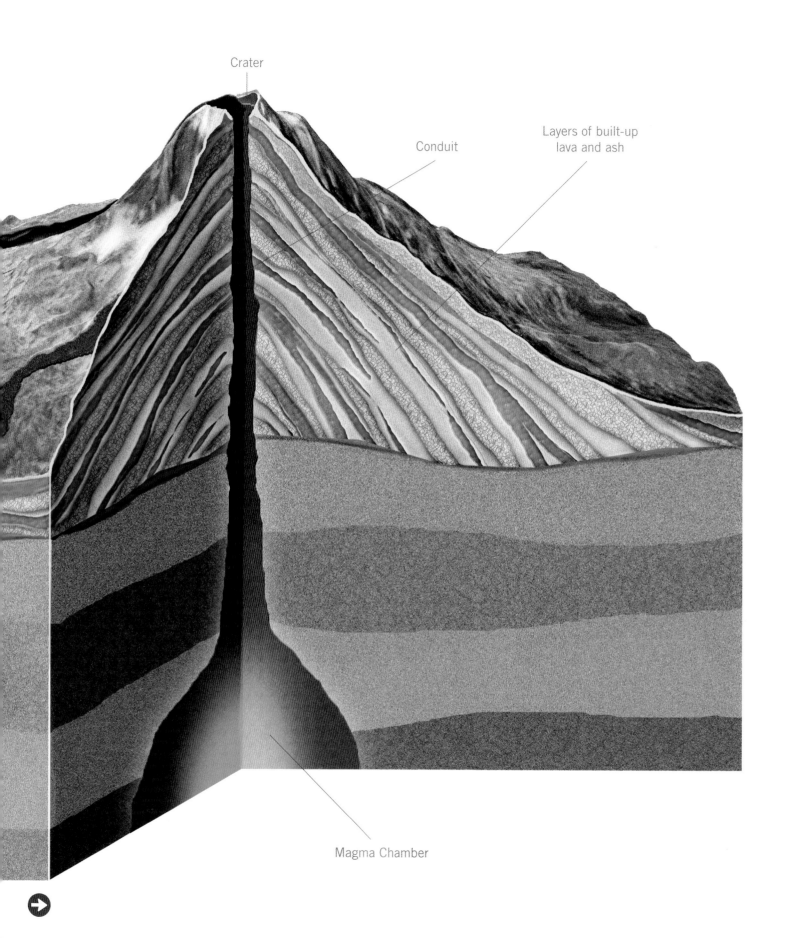

Crater

Conduit

Layers of built-up
lava and ash

Magma Chamber

Cinder Cone Volcano

A steep-sided cinder cone volcano rises a few hundred feet above the surrounding land. It is the result of violent eruptions that blast gobs of thick, sticky lava and chunks of rock into the air. The materials land near the crater and cool quickly to form the cone.

Composite Volcano

A composite volcano forms when periods of quiet, continuous eruptions are followed by violent blasts. Over time, layer after layer of material builds up to form steep-sided, cone-shaped slopes.

Caldera Volcano

A caldera volcano has a broad, shallow crater that forms when a tremendous explosion partially collapses the top of the volcano. If more volcanic activity occurs after the collapse, new volcanic hills or mountains may form inside the crater and rise up to form a new mountaintop.

Mauna Loa, Hawaii

3

Zao, Okama, Miyagi, Japan

4

Paricutin, Mexico

5

ROCK ON!

When Lava Cools

When lava gushes out of a volcano, it's a sizzling 1,300 to 2,200°F (700 to 1,200°C). That's six to ten times hotter than boiling water! But the instant lava hits air or water, it starts to cool. In as little as a few minutes, it hardens into solid rock.

There are many kinds of volcanic rock on Earth. Each kind has different properties and uses depending on the materials in the lava and how quickly it cooled. Some of the most interesting kinds of volcanic rock are described below.

Obsidian

Obsidian is a shiny volcanic glass. Because it forms when lava cools very quickly, there is not enough time for crystals to form in the rock. That is why flakes break off obsidian rock easily. Native American peoples used obsidian to make tools and weapons, such as arrowheads. Other early peoples used it to make masks, mirrors, and jewelry.

Basalt

Basalt is the most common volcanic rock on Earth. It covers all of the world's seafloors. Basalt forms from thin, runny lava. Most of the roads and parking lots in the United States are paved with crushed basalt because it is widely available, inexpensive, and stands up well to heavy traffic.

ROCK ON!

When Lava Cools

When lava gushes out of a volcano, it's a sizzling 1,300 to 2,200°F (700 to 1,200°C). That's six to ten times hotter than boiling water! But the instant lava hits air or water, it starts to cool. In as little as a few minutes, it hardens into solid rock.

There are many kinds of volcanic rock on Earth. Each kind has different properties and uses depending on the materials in the lava and how quickly it cooled. Some of the most interesting kinds of volcanic rock are described below.

Obsidian

Obsidian is a shiny volcanic glass. Because it forms when lava cools very quickly, there is not enough time for crystals to form in the rock. That is why flakes break off obsidian rock easily. Native American peoples used obsidian to make tools and weapons, such as arrowheads. Other early peoples used it to make masks, mirrors, and jewelry.

Basalt

Basalt is the most common volcanic rock on Earth. It covers all of the world's seafloors. Basalt forms from thin, runny lava. Most of the roads and parking lots in the United States are paved with crushed basalt because it is widely available, inexpensive, and stands up well to heavy traffic.

Mauna Loa, Hawaii

3

Zao, Okama, Miyagi, Japan

4

Paricutin, Mexico

5

Volcanic Landscapes

The broad, rolling plains, towering mountains, and vast canyons we see on Earth today provide clues about our planet's past. Just like the erosion caused by wind and water, volcanic blasts and lava flows have created the land features that surround us.

Devils Tower

Devils Tower was once the central core of a volcano. Over time, the surrounding rock slowly eroded to reveal this amazing structure. Today Devils Tower rises 1,267 feet (386 m) above the Wyoming plains.

Black Beaches

In places such as the Hawaiian Islands, Scotland, New Zealand, and Greece, tourists enjoy vast basalt beaches made of tiny grains of rock that came from volcanoes. The beautiful beach in this photo is located on the north coast of Hawai'i.

Pumice

Pumice is a lightweight rock full of tiny holes. The lava from which it formed was a bubbly froth of gases and magma. It is used to make everything from concrete and heavy-duty cleaners to toothpaste and pencil erasers.

Rhyolite

Rhyolite is a common volcanic rock that forms from thick, sticky lava. Hells Canyon, on the Idaho-Oregon border, has hundreds of towering rhyolite columns. The rock was formed following volcanic eruptions that occurred about 17 million years ago. Over the last 6 million years, the mighty Snake River slowly carved out a path and exposed the rock columns. The river flows more than a mile below the canyon's west rim, making it the deepest river gorge in North America.

The Andes Mountains

Many of the world's mountains form as lava spills out of the crust, cools, hardens, and slowly piles up. The Andes Mountains, the longest continental mountain chain on Earth, are located along the western coast of South America. They form the eastern edge of the Pacific Ring of Fire. As the Nazca and Antarctic Plates crash into the South American Plate, eruptions along the Andean Volcanic Belt spew tons of ash and lava onto Earth's surface. The Andes are made of a gray, fine-grained volcanic rock called andesite. It is the second most common volcanic rock on Earth.

Fertile Fields

As rain and snow slowly eroded the surface of this extinct volcano in Rwanda, minerals from the bits and pieces of rock formed rich soil that is perfect for farming. Today local peoples grow acre after acre of wheat along the volcano's slopes and inside its crater.

SIZING UP VOLCANOES

What Is VEI?

About five hundred different volcanoes have erupted on Earth since people began keeping written records. Each year, between fifty and sixty volcanoes ooze, gush, or blast lava and other materials, but only a few of them cause major damage to the surrounding land.

To measure and compare the strength and size of volcanic eruptions, scientists use a scale called the Volcanic Explosivity Index (VEI). It was developed by Chris Newhall and Steve Self in 1982. The VEI ranks blasts from 0 to 8, with eruptions that consist of gently flowing lava ranking a 0 and the most violent blasts receiving an 8. Each number on the scale represents an eruption ten times more severe than the preceding number.

How do scientists assign a VEI value to an eruption? First, they consider the amount and type of material released, the height of the ash cloud, and how long the eruption lasts. Then they factor in their personal observations of the blast.

Lift the flap on the next page to learn more about the Volcanic Explosivity Index.

Volcanologist Chris Newall taking samples at Mount Pinatubo in the Philippines shortly after its 1991 eruption.

Mega-Blasts!

By studying rocks, scientists have found evidence of several mega-colossal eruptions that occurred long ago. One of them took place about 640,000 years ago in what is now Yellowstone National Park.

4	Large	6–16 miles (10–25 km)	Vulcanian/ Plinian	359	Chaitén, Chile, 2008
3	Moderate to large	2–9 miles (3–15 km)	Vulcanian	990	Nevado del Ruiz, Colombia, 1985
2	Moderate	3,300– 16,500 feet (1,000– 5,000 m)	Strombolian/ Vulcanian	3,756	Ruapehu, New Zealand, 1971
1	Gentle	330– 3,300 feet (100– 1,000 m)	Hawaiian/ Strombolian	Many	Poás, Costa Rica, 1990
0	Non-explosive	Less than 330 feet (100 m)	Hawaiian	Many	Mauna Loa, Hawaii

BLASTS FROM THE PAST

Mount Tambora

Where: Sumbawa, Indonesia
When: April 5 to July 15, 1815
Why: Indo-Australian Plate colliding with Eurasian Plate
VEI: 7

Mount Tambora once rose 14,000 feet (4,270 m) into the sky, but today it is less than 10,000 feet (3,050 m) tall. That's because the giant composite volcano blew its top about 200 years ago.

At the height of the eruption, gases and debris rocketed 27 miles (43 km) into the air. Ash and dust blocked out the sun, creating an eerie darkness that lasted for three days. Thousands of homes collapsed under the weight of ash, lapilli, and volcanic bombs that rained down for about two weeks after the major blast on April 15, 1815.

The blast killed ten thousand people within minutes. Only twenty-six people on Sumbawa survived. At least eighty thousand additional people died on nearby islands because their homes and crops were buried by ash and other other volcanic materials.

I Was There!

The Mount Tambora eruption spewed so much gas and ash into the sky that it blocked sunlight all over the world. The following winter was freezing cold, and people in North America and Europe called 1816 "the year without a summer."

A June storm blanketed some parts of New England with 1.5 feet (0.5 m) of snow. In Plymouth, Connecticut, farmer Chauncey Jerome wrote that ". . . on the 10th of June, my wife brought in the washing frozen stiff. . . . On the 4th of July, I saw several men . . . in the middle of the day with thick coats on." Because farmers couldn't grow crops that year, at least 100,000 people died of starvation.

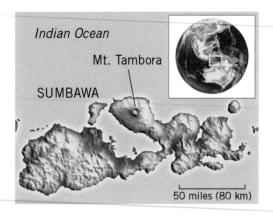

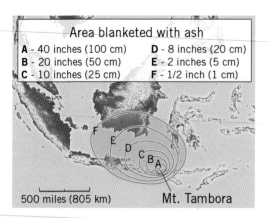

Area blanketed with ash
A - 40 inches (100 cm) D - 8 inches (20 cm)
B - 20 inches (50 cm) E - 2 inches (5 cm)
C - 10 inches (25 cm) F - 1/2 inch (1 cm)

During the 1815 eruption of Mount Tambora, land up to 559 miles (900 km) from the volcano was blanketed with ash.

Volcanic Explosivity Index (VEI)

VEI	Description	Height of Blast	Type of Eruption	Number Recorded in Last 10,000 Years	Example
8	Mega-colossal	More than 16 miles (25 km)	Ultra-Plinian	0	Taupo, New Zealand, 26,560 years ago
7	Super-colossal	More than 16 miles (25 km)	Plinian/ Ultra-Plinian	7	Tambora, Indonesia, 1815
6	Colossal	More than 16 miles (25 km)	Plinian/ Ultra-Plinian	48	Pinatubo, Philippines, 1991
5	Very large	More than 16 miles (25 km)	Plinian	122	Saint Helens, United States, 1980

Biggest Isn't Always Baddest

The 1815 eruption of Mount Tambora on Sumbawa, an island in Indonesia, was the most explosive blast in the last 10,000 years, so it's no surprise that it killed many people. But big blasts don't always do the most damage. In fact, some of the deadliest eruptions in history ranked low on the VEI scale. The 1985 eruption of Nevado del Ruiz in Colombia received a VEI score of 3. Why was it the fourth deadliest blast of all time? Heat from the eruption melted ice and snow at the top of the cone-shaped mountain, triggering a mudflow that buried an entire village and killed all the people living in it.

The Ten Deadliest Eruptions in Recorded History

Volcano	Location	Number of People Killed	VEI	Date
Tambora	Indonesia	92,000	7	1815
Krakatau	Indonesia	36,000	6	1883
Pelée	Martinique	29,000	4	1902
Nevado del Ruiz	Colombia	23,000	3	1985
Unzen	Japan	14,300	2	1792
Kelut	Indonesia	10,000	5	1586
Santa Maria	Guatemala	10,000	6	1902
Laki	Iceland	9,300	6	1783
Kelut	Indonesia	5,500	4	1919
Galunggung	Indonesia	4,000	4	1882

A Traffic Stopper

The 2010 eruption of Eyjafjallajökull (say AYE-ya-fyah-dla-JOW-kudl) in Iceland scored a 4 on the VEI scale and it didn't kill a single person, but that doesn't mean it didn't cause trouble. For 6 days, so much ash filled the sky above Europe that airplanes couldn't fly. Close to 100,000 flights were cancelled, trapping travelers and crippling many international businesses.

On June 3, 2009, astronauts onboard the International Space Station snapped this dramatic photo of Mount Tambora's 3.7-mile (6-km) wide crater. The 3,600-foot (1,100 m) deep hole is the telltale scar of the most violent blast in recorded history. Today, the crater floor features a freshwater lake, minor lava flows, and layers of material deposited by the 1815 eruption.

Before

During

Six months before Mount St. Helens's devastating eruption in 1980, its mighty peak showed no sign of the fiery storm brewing inside the volcano.

Mount St. Helens

Where: Washington, United States

When: May 18, 1980

Why: North American Plate colliding
with the Juan de Fuca Plate,
a small plate at the eastern edge
of the Pacific Ring of Fire

VEI: 6

In the 1960s and 1970s, Mount St. Helens was a popular vacation spot. People enjoyed hiking and camping in the beautiful forests along its slopes. But in 1978, the United States Geographical Survey (USGS) warned that the composite volcano might erupt by the end of the century. Little did they know that the worst volcanic disaster in U.S. history was only two years away.

In March 1980, the volcano started to come to life. Earthquakes shook the area. Steam and ash shot out of vents near the top. Over the next few weeks, the northern slope bulged as magma forced its way to the surface. In April 1980, volcanologist David Johnson told reporters, "We're standing next to a dynamite keg and the fuse is lit. We just don't know how long the fuse is. I'm genuinely afraid of it." Johnson and other scientists predicted that the volcano would erupt soon—and they were right.

On May 18, an intense earthquake shook Mount St. Helens, setting off a chain of events that transformed the scenic mountaintop into a gray, dusty wasteland. First, the unstable north side collapsed. It triggered an explosion and landslide that devastated an area the size of Chicago, Illinois. Ash, steam, and gas blasted upward and sideways, traveling 300 miles (482 km) per hour. Anything in the path of destruction didn't stand a chance.

After 9 hours, the eruptions finally stopped. They had ripped enough material off the mountain to lower its height by 1,300 feet (397 m). Millions of trees were blown down by the force of the gases spewing out of the volcano and nearly fifty thousand animals died. Heat from the gases and ash started forest fires that burned for months.

But that wasn't the end of the story. During the 1980s, Mount St. Helens erupted at least fifteen more times. These blasts weren't as large or destructive, but they blanketed nearby towns with ash.

Many animals have returned to the mountain, and new trees are growing. But scientists say the recovery process will take 200 to 500 years.

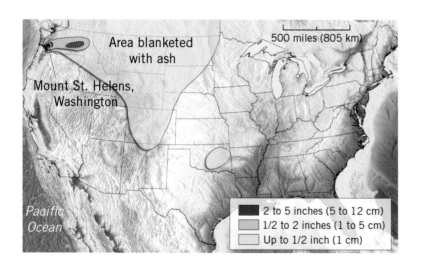

Ash Everywhere

Following the eruption of Mount St. Helens, several inches of ash covered everything for miles around.

The ash Mount St. Helens spewed during its 1980 eruption traveled high into the atmosphere and spread over a large area of the United States. Scientists detected bits of volcanic fallout in eleven states. The ash traveled as far east as Minnesota and as far south as Oklahoma.

Mount Pinatubo

Where: Luzon, Philippines
When: June 12 to 15, 1991
Why: Eurasian Plate colliding with the Philippine Sea Plate, a small plate at the western edge of the Pacific Ring of Fire
VEI: 6

In April 1991, Mount Pinatubo suddenly started belching steam. Even though the volcano hadn't erupted in six hundred years, scientists rushed to Luzon.

During the next few weeks, small earthquakes shook the area. This was a sure sign that the area was becoming unstable and an eruption could occur at any time. In early June, scientists convinced officials to evacuate eighty thousand people from the area.

On June 12, the volcano erupted, spewing tons of ash and gases into the air. "[The cloud was] bigger than anything I'd ever seen before, and it was moving really fast . . . it was kind of terrifying," recalls American geophysicist Andy Lockhart.

That was just the beginning! The eruptions kept coming every few hours, and each one was more powerful. Following the final blast on June 15, ash and pumice rained down over an area the size of Arizona. It was the second most explosive eruption of the twentieth century.

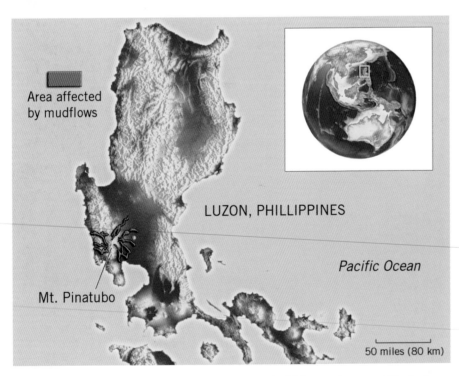

Area affected by mudflows

LUZON, PHILLIPINES

Pacific Ocean

Mt. Pinatubo

50 miles (80 km)

Because scientists warned officials in time, only 320 people were killed when Mount Pinatubo erupted in 1991. Most of them died when buildings collapsed under the weight of ash. Unfortunately, a typhoon struck Luzon during the blast. Rain from the storm turned volcanic ash into mud, causing mudflows that killed at least 600 people and left 100,000 people homeless.

I Was There!

In 1991, Cora K. lived about 20 miles (32 km) from Mount Pinatubo. When the blast darkened the sky at noon, Cora "thought it was going to be the end of the world."

"At first, powerful earthquakes began shaking the ground. As the volcano was erupting, it was spitting thick ashes into the air. Then, volcanic ashes began falling on everything."

After the volcano settled down, "The ashes were knee deep," said Cora. "It was hard to walk, and it was hard to breathe. The ashes would stick to your hair and your skin . . . It took months to clean up."

During the 1991 Mount Pinatubo eruption, ash, gases, and rock were thrust 25 miles (40 km) into the air. This picture shows a jeep speeding away from the blast.

The ash that rains down during and after a volcanic eruption can look just like a massive snowstorm. During an eruption on May 25, 1980, Robert Emetaz was caught driving directly into the ashfall. When the early morning rain became muddy, he realized "we were having another eruption. The sky, rather than getting lighter as the morning progressed, got darker. . . and darker. It was like the middle of the night." In the inky blankness, damaged powerlines sparked around Emetaz like lightning bolts.

After

I Was There!

The Mount St. Helens eruption killed fifty-seven people, but U.S. Forest Service technician Kathy Pearson managed to survive. She was camping with friends 15 miles (24 km) north of the mountain. "All of us [thought] we were dead," she said. "[T]he cloud just kept getting bigger and bigger and bigger and the lightning was fierce, just unbelievable. The clouds ... roared and boiled and it was very, very terrifying."

VOLCANO SCIENTISTS IN ACTION

Before a Blast

Scientists started studying Hawaii's gently-erupting volcanoes in the early 1900s, but it wasn't until they monitored the explosive blasts at Mount St. Helens and Mount Pinatubo that they began to understand the true complexity of volcanoes. They found that every volcano is different. Because the forces that cause volcanic activity are at work deep below Earth's surface, it's hard to know exactly when an eruption will occur and how destructive it will be. Still, scientists keep trying because predicting volcanoes can save lives.

To learn about a volcano, scientists gather data. They study the surrounding landscape to discover how often and how violently the volcano has erupted in the past. They scramble up steep slopes and climb into craters to observe the structure of volcanoes and collect rock samples. They set up equipment that measures earthquake activity and detects temperature changes inside the crater. Then they return to their labs and analyze all the information for clues.

Volcanologists Chris Newhall and Arturo Daag exploring the crater of Mount Pinatubo in the Philippines.

Scientists monitor the 2002 eruption of Guagua Pichincha in Ecuador. The volcano's central vent belched gases and ash for 8 days.

VOLCANO WATCH

In the weeks leading up to Mount St. Helens's eruption, scientists observed the volcano day and night to learn more about it and the steps leading up to a major eruption. They also collected and studied ash spewing out of the crater. All this information helped the researchers understand volcanoes better than ever before. Here are some of field notes written by scientist Rick Hoblitt during an overnight watch:

• •

7:53 P.M.	Almost total darkness. Set out coffee can ash sampler with coffee filter paper.
9:25 P.M.	Explosions. Earthquakes. Rain continues heavy.
10:27 P.M..	Quake—pretty strong.
2:20 A.M.	Summit visible. No rain.
2:22 A.M.	Weak [eruptive] activity.
2:26 A.M.	Continues, appears ash rich. Could be moving down north or northeast from summit.
2:53 A.M.	Mild activity at summit and clouds barely above summit.
6:26 A.M.	Activity apparent, ash rich plume.
6:48 A.M.	Emission subsides.
8:47 A.M.	No summit observations possible since last entry, cloud cover now down to Timberline.
8:50 A.M.	Raining [very hard].

• •

Will it Erupt?

When a volcano erupts, scientists really go to work. During gentle eruptions, scientists may put on bulky, heat-resistant suits and study lava up close. They measure its temperature and observe how it cools.

Scientists monitor more explosive blasts with aircraft and satellites. They may film lava flows and gas clouds from a safe distance. After the blast, they may don hard hats and special gloves, and hike around the volcano's slopes and crater.

Thanks to all this hard work, scientists have identified three signs that tell an eruption will occur soon:
- an increase in earthquake activity
- an increase in gas emissions
- the surface of the volcano swells

If all three of these signs occur, people living nearby are warned to evacuate.

This scientist's fire-resistant suit protects him from the 2,093° F (1,145° C) lava spilling out of Mauna Loa in Hawai'i.

ASH AROUND THE WORLD

Following the 1991 eruption of Mount Pinatubo, scientists studied how its ash and gases moved through Earth's atmosphere. After just two months, a thin cloud of ash circled the entire planet. Because the material reflected some of the sun's heat back into space, the entire planet cooled about 1° F (0.6° C) over the next 15 months. That's when scientists realized that the Mount Tambora eruption in 1815 had cooled Earth enough to cause "the year without a summer."

Now some scientists think we should add particles that act like ash to the atmosphere. They say it could slow down—or even stop—global warming. Other scientists think it's a bad idea to introduce new materials into the atmosphere. They are worried that the particles might cause new problems that we can't even predict.

This stunning view of ash belching out of Chaiten Volcano in Chile was captured on January 19, 2009, by ASTER, a special imaging instrument circling Earth onboard the Terra satellite.

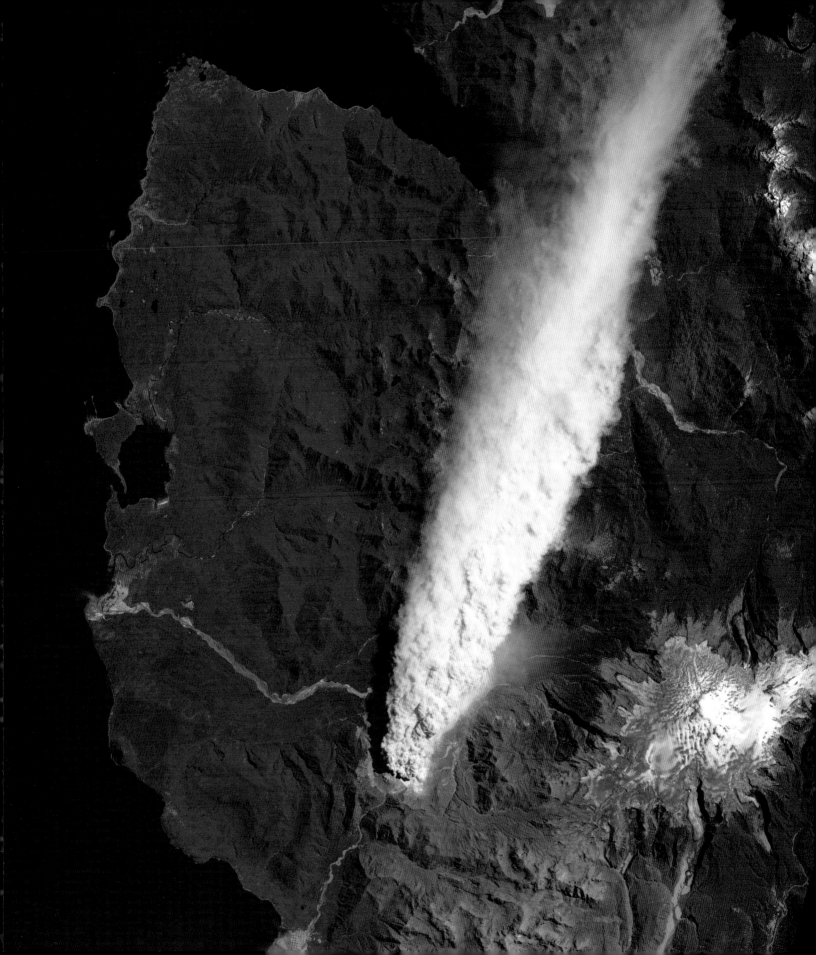

Undersea Volcanoes

When towering volcanic mountains, such as Tambora, Pinatubo, and St. Helens, blow their tops, people pay a lot of attention. But each year, there are dozens of eruptions that most people don't even notice. That's because they happen far below the ocean's wavy surface.

Scientists worked for many years to map the ocean floor. When they finally finished the job, they were surprised to see a network of undersea volcanic ridges that crisscrosses Earth's underwater surface. With all those volcanoes, it's no wonder that 90 percent of Earth's volcanic activity occurs in the ocean.

It turns out undersea volcanoes are located in places where Earth's plates are moving apart. As the plates travel in opposite directions, magma rises to the surface and slowly spills out. When the lava comes into contact with the chilly ocean waters, it cools quickly and forms new seafloor.

Believe It or Not

The longest mountain chain on Earth winds its way across the seafloor. It is more than 40,000 miles (64,000 kilometers) long and includes ridges with names like the Mid-Atlantic Ridge, the East Pacific Rise, and the Southwest Indian Ridge.

The yellow lines on this map show the location of undersea volcanic ridges. The ridges form in places where Earth's plates are slowly moving away from one another.

Volcanoes in Space

Earth isn't the only place in space with volcanoes. In fact, there's a mountain of evidence to support the idea that volcanoes can be found on the Moon, Mercury, Venus, Mars, and some of the moons in the outer solar system. Let's take a look at some volcanoes that are out of this world. Scientists are learning more about them every day.

Moon

There are no active volcanoes on the Moon today, but there were billions of years ago. When you look at the Moon from Earth, you see lighter and darker regions. The darker regions are vast plains of rock that formed when lava spilled onto the Moon's surface and slowly cooled.

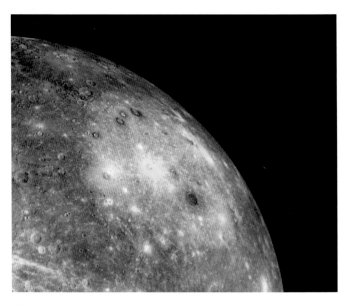

Mercury

In 2010, scientists announced that NASA's Messenger spacecraft had captured stunning images proving that Mercury was once home to dozens of active volcanoes. It even spotted a large, double-ringed basin with a smooth floor that must have been formed by an ancient lava flow.

Venus

The surface of our closest neighboring planet is 90 percent basalt, and scientists have spotted signs of recent lava flows. That's no surprise, because more than 100,000 volcanoes dot Venus's surface. The largest is a shield volcano named Maat Mons.

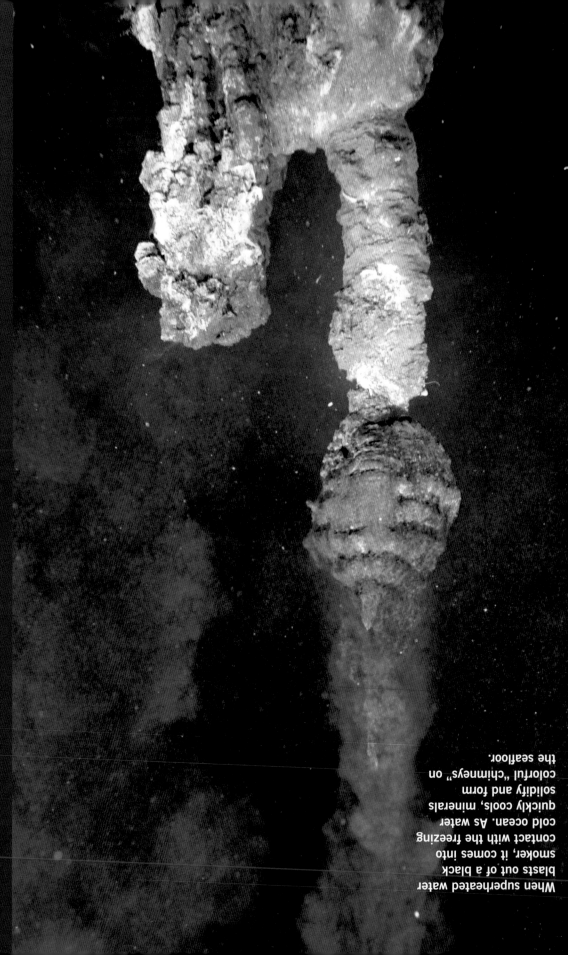

BLACK SMOKERS

Sometimes chilly seawater leaks into undersea volcanoes. As the water is superheated by magma, it picks up minerals from the surrounding rocks. Then it blasts into the ocean as smoky steam. Scientists call the spewing material and the vents through which it escapes black smokers. Scientists study black smokers because the heat and minerals they release into the deep sea can fuel entire communities of bizarre creatures. Imagine clams the size of dinner plates, sea jellies that look like dandelions, and tall, red-topped tubeworms that gently sway in the ocean currents. Scientists have seen all these animals living around black smokers.

When superheated water blasts out of a black smoker, it comes into contact with the freezing cold ocean. As water quickly cools, minerals solidify and form colorful "chimneys" on the seafloor.

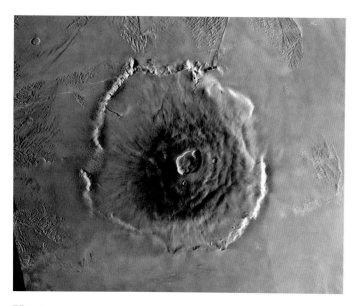

Mars

The red planet is home to huge shield volcanoes that have been extinct for millions of years. The largest, Olympus Mons, rises 17 miles (27 km) above the surface. Its base covers an area the size of Arizona.

Jupiter

The king of the planets has a gassy surface, but its closest moon, Io, shows clear signs of volcanic activity. In fact, spacecraft have captured images of blasts in progress. Scientists believe friction caused by the gravitation pull of Jupiter causes Io's eruptions.

Neptune

Spacecraft have also spotted blasts in progress on Triton, one of Neptune's moons. Scientists think the plumes come from ice volcanoes that spout liquid nitrogen, dust, and methane compounds into the moon's atmosphere.

Words to Know

conduit a long tube that connects a volcano's magma chamber to its crater

core the center of Earth. The inner core is solid, and the outer core is liquid.

crater the part of a volcano through which lava spills

crust the outer layer of Earth

earthquake a series of vibrations that radiates through Earth's interior

emission materials, such as ash from a volcano, released into the air

hotspot a place where magma spikes through Earth's crust in the middle of a plate

magma hot, soft rock that makes up Earth's mantle. When mantle spills onto the surface, it is called lava.

magma chamber the area inside a volcano where magma is stored prior to an eruption

mantle the layer of Earth between the crust and outer core. It is made of soft rock called magma.

plate one of the large slabs of rock that makes up Earth's crust

volcano a crack or hole in Earth's surface that extends through the crust and into the mantle. The word may also be used to describe the mountain of hardened lava that forms around the crack.

Find Out More

Websites to Visit

Mount St. Helens VolcanoCam
www.fs.fed.us/gpnf/volcanocams/msh/

Smithsonian Institution Global Volcanism Program
http://www.volcano.si.edu/gvp

This Dynamic Planet
www.minerals.si.edu/tdpmap/

Volcano World
volcano.und.nodak.edu/vw.html

Books to Read

Volcanoes: Eyewitness to Disaster by Judy and Dennis Fradin (National Geographic, 2007).

Forces of Nature by Catherine O'Neill Grace (National Geographic, 2004).

Into the Volcano by Donna O'Meara (Two Can Press, 2005).

Earthquakes and Volcanoes by Alison Rae (Smart Apple Media, 2006).

Earthquakes and Volcanoes by Melissa Stewart (HarperCollins, 2008).

Bibliography

Beals, Herbert K., Scott Kline, and Julie M. Kole. *On the Mountain's Brink: A Forest Service History of the 1980 Mount St. Helens Volcanic Emergency.* Washington, DC: United States Forest Service, 1981.

de Boer, Jelle Zeilinga and Donald Theodore Sanders. *Volcanoes in Human History: The Far-Reaching Effects of Major Eruptions.* Princeton, NJ: Princeton University Press, 2004.

Fradin, Judy and Dennis. *Volcanoes: Eyewitness to Disaster.* Washington, D.C.: National Geographic, 2007.

O'Meara, Donna. *Volcano: A Visual Guide.* New York: Firefly Books, 2008.

Rosi, Mauro, Paolo Paple, Luca Lupi, and Marco Stoppato. *Volcanoes.* New York: Firefly Books, 2003.

Scarth, Alwyn. *Vulcan's Fury: Man Against the Volcano.* New Haven, CT: Yale University Press, 1999.

Stommel, Henry and Elizabeth Stommel. *Volcano Weather: The Story of 1816, the Year Without a Summer.* Newport, RI: Seven Seas Pres, Inc., 1983.

Thompson, Dick. *Volcano Cowboys: The Rocky Evolution of a Dangerous Science.* New York: St. Martin's Press, 2000.

Tilling, Robert I. *Eruptions of Mount St. Helens: Past, Present, and Future.* Washington, DC: United States Geographical Survey, 1990.

Williams, Stanley and Fen Montaigne. *Surviving Galeras.* Boston: Houghton Mifflin, 2001.

Source Notes

Page 30: ". . . on the 10th . . . thick coats on." Stanley Williams and Fen Montaigne. *Surviving Galeras.* (Houghton Mifflin, 2001).

Page 32: "The cloud was . . . it was kind of terrifying." Dick Thompson. *Volcano Cowboys: The Rocky Evolution of a Dangerous Science.* (St. Martin's Press, 2000).

Page 32: "thought is was . . . to clean up." "Escaping Mount Pinatubo" *Weekly Reader Online.* www.weeklyreader.com/featurezone/eyewitness/eyewitness_2.asp (Accessed January 8, 2010).

Page 33: "We're standing next . . . afraid of it." "Volcano Cleared Its Throat 5 Years Ago." *The Spokesman-Review*, March 24, 1985.

Page 35: "All of us . . . very, very terrifying." Herbert K. Beals, Scott Kline, and Julie M. Kole. *On the Mountain's Brink: A Forest Service History of the 1980 Mount St. Helens Volcanic Emergency.* (United States Forest Service, 1981).

Page 36: "we were having . . . of the night." Beals, Herbert K., Scott Kline, and Julie M. Kole. *On the Mountain's Brink: A Forest Service History of the 1980 Mount St. Helens Volcanic Emergency.* (United States Forest Service, 1981), p. 44.

Page 39: "7:53 p.m. Almost total darkness . . . Raining [very hard]." Dick Thompson. *Volcano Cowboys: The Rocky Evolution of a Dangerous Science.* (St. Martin's Press, 2000).

Index